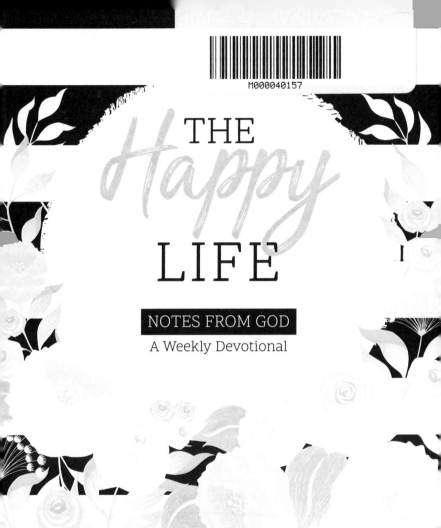

THE Happy LIFE

NOTES FROM GOD

A Weekly Devotional

Drenda Keesee

The Happy Life
Notes From God
A Weekly Devotional

ISBN: 978-1-945930-05-8

Published by Free Indeed Publishers.
Distributed by Drenda Keesee Ministries.

Drenda Keesee Ministries
P.O. Box 647
New Albany, OH 43054

You can reach Drenda Keesee Ministries on the Internet at www.drenda.com.

THE Happy LIFE

A Weekly Devotional

Drenda Keesee

Dedication

This book is dedicated to YOU and your journey toward a happier and healthier life!

Happiness means whole relationships, peace, rest, provision, and achieving your dreams; and I believe this devotional is going to help you get there. Thank you for the time you put in every day in your relentless pursuit for God. You are making a difference!

"I am bringing you out, and the pathway to that promotion is to bring you through… through situations you think are insurmountable, pressure you feel inadequate to navigate. I don't bring the pressure; I bring you through the pressure. Your trust is being forged in the battle to make you an indestructible treasure of my own mastery. Don't be discouraged, but rather, encouraged that you are being formed, and the outcome will be praiseworthy! When we are finished with this journey, you will resemble me more than ever, and that is what you have asked."

Week One

Happy Thoughts

"Then you will know the truth, and the truth will set you free."
—John 8:32 (NIV)

Do you feel like you spend a lot of time dwelling on the negatives? Oftentimes, we let our circumstances overwhelm us. We focus on the moment and forget that there is something bigger and better ahead of us.

My husband, Gary, and I spent the early years of our marriage in an old farmhouse. There was a season that I got stuck thinking about the negative things: the ancient appliances; the wild plants pushing their way through the windows; the testy, turn-of-the-century toilet—the only one in the whole house! While living in that small farmhouse, we went through difficult times. We didn't have any money or even the hope of having any money. Believe me, I reached for anger, and when that didn't work, I reached for self-pity—but I realized that dwelling on negative thoughts was robbing me of my joy. I knew I needed to break that cycle of defeat, so I put a sign in the bathroom that read:

Make the Choice to Rejoice.

You always have a choice: Focus on yesterday's pain or today's joy. God brought us out of that farmhouse, but the lessons I learned there, I still carry with me today. Life can be difficult.

You can choose joy by seeking out God's Word! God's Word is an anchor for your soul. If you just open your ears to God's voice, He will shatter those chains of negativity and speak His truth into your heart.

God loves you; He has wonderful things in store for you! Repeat the words in Psalm 139: "I praise you, for I am fearfully and wonderfully made. Wonderful are your works; my soul knows it very well."

NOTES

_____

_____

_____

_____

_____

_____

_____

_____

_____

_____

"*I* created marriage and I know how to unlock its joys. As you sharpen one another, there is more room for my blessing—so don't resent the gift of another person's perspective as the agent to help present you to me glorious without spot, wrinkle, or blemish at my return. Learn to love with my love and answer with my tone."

Week Two

The Power of Agreement

"Therefore having put away falsehood, let each one of you speak the truth with his neighbor, for we are members of one another. Be angry and do not sin; do not let the sun go down on your anger, and give no opportunity to the devil."

—Ephesians 4:25-27 (ESV)

Some men watch football. Some build things with their hands. My husband, he loves the great outdoors. If you could only see how his face lights up when he pulls on his camouflage, throws his bow over his shoulder, and marches out into the brisk open air. I love to see that expression on his face—but I didn't always.

I used to think all hunters were backwards hillbillies—needless to say, marrying one was never on my five-year plan! Then I met and fell in love with Gary, and I knew I had to come to terms with this whole hunting thing. I just didn't get it: You climb a tree, it's 5:00 in the morning, it smells like deer excrement, and you have to sit there for hours. How was that fun?

In our early days of marriage, it was... a struggle. There were times when I wanted his help around the house and he wanted to go hunting. It wasn't only hunting, though; suddenly, we were disagreeing on a lot, and neither one of us was willing to see the situation from the other person's perspective. Strife is a dangerous game you don't want to play. You may win the argument, but strife comes at a high cost. It opens the door to the enemy, robs you of your peace, and short-circuits God's access into your life. It's no wonder we spent nine years living hand-to-mouth, drowning in financial chaos.

Gary and I learned a critical lesson the hard way: You can't have success until you learn how to live together in unity. Understanding the power of agreement was a complete paradigm shift for us. When we'd start to get into an argument, we'd turn to each other and say, "I'd rather prosper." I started to value hunting as a hobby that was important to Gary, instead of marking it off as a waste of time. And he began to look for ways to help me around the house.

The enemy loves to get into marriages and cause division, which is why husbands and wives need to encourage each other and work together to bring about God's plan. Faith gives us a common vision; without that vision, marriages won't succeed. In agreement, we have the victory. What awesome power there is in a united marriage!

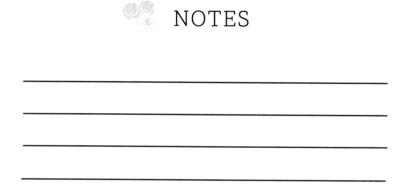 NOTES

_____

_____

_____

_____

"*O*ften it is the little things that are truly the big things. My children hear my voice and follow it, and your family will do the same if you build time into your schedule for them to hear your voice and experience your love. This is the foundation that brings encouragement and growth."

Week Three
Refocused

"Train up a child in the way he should go; even when he is old he will not depart from it."
—Proverbs 22:6 (ESV)

Our daily lives are full of distractions and pressures: paying bills, running errands, driving the kids to practice. The enemy would love nothing more than for us to go into survival mode and live in a constant state of frantic busyness. When you only focus on the earthly concerns, stress inevitably creeps in, and stress can cause conflict. So how do we stop letting today's worries steal tomorrow's joy and begin to see God's plan for our lives?

Listening.

Allow God to reveal answers to you. When God speaks to you, it's up to you to listen and obey His Word. Financial worries, work issues, and overly busy schedules will add pressure to your family, creating cracks in your foundation. When this happens, we get off the path God wants us to follow. You can change your course by making God and family your top priorities!

Switch from surviving to thriving.

At least once a week, put everything else aside and focus on your family. Go for a walk together. Pop some popcorn and watch a movie. Play a board game, even if your kids complain that it's not as fun as their smartphones! Just as Jesus was the Good Shepherd for us, so too we must do our part to shepherd our children and be an example of love to them.

NOTES

_____

_____

_____

_____

_____

_____

_____

_____

_____

_____

_____

_____

"When your children or beloved go astray, everything in you longs for them to return. So is my heart toward mine. I have called you to demonstrate my forgiveness and let me take care of the rest. Don't fret over whether you will get your share of blessings. My kingdom does not require someone to lose for you to win. Lack of faith and trust in my goodness fuel division, competitive jealousy, and gossip. If you knew how much I have to give, you would never worry about being left out or try to make someone less to make you more. Be sure there is a day of judgment coming, but this is not it."

Week Four

Trusting God

"Judge not, that you be not judged. For with the judgment you pronounce you will be judged, and with the measure you use it will be measured to you."
—Matthew 7:1-2 (ESV)

It can be easy to slip into judgment, even with good intentions. Understanding judgment is the key to stopping it. So what is judgment, really? At the heart of this dangerously contagious mind-set lies self-righteousness.

"I can't believe they did that! I would *never*. I'm nothing like them!" See how easy that is?

The truth is, we've *all* sinned and fallen short of the life God has called us to live. The Bible encourages us to reach for love and understanding when we're tempted to judge. Empathy is our secret weapon against this wrong mind-set!

So what is empathy?

Empathy simply means stepping into someone else's shoes—remembering that we've made mistakes, that we're all human, and recognizing how we would want to be treated if the roles were reversed. That sounds easy enough, right? Unfortunately, it's harder than it sounds. Empathizing with someone is a courageous act—a selfless, vulnerable undertaking.

We have to put down our judgment and arm ourselves with compassion and empathy. Think about the way Jesus reacted when He encountered Martha and Mary after the death of their brother, Lazarus. Jesus didn't break out the pom-poms to try to lift their spirits, or dust off some old jokes to lighten the mood. He didn't say, "Well, it could be worse." How many of us have heard that one?

What did Jesus do? John 11:35 says, "Jesus wept."

Jesus shed tears right beside the grieving family. When Jesus wept, that was God baring Himself, showing us that He understands and empathizes with our struggle.

Not only does God understand our pain, He draws near to us and feels it with us. Imagine how much He loves us!

 NOTES

_____

_____

_____

_____

_____

_____

_____

GOD NOTE

"*I* am waiting to spend time with you and share my secret kingdom."

WEEK FIVE

Silence is Golden

"And rising very early in the morning, while it was still dark, he [Jesus] departed and went out to a desolate place, and there he prayed."
—MARK 1:35 (ESV)

People are social. We love to get together and talk, and those times should be celebrated. But how often do you spend time talking to God?

One of the most powerful habits you can cultivate is valuing and protecting your time with God. When you get up in the morning, what's the first thing you do? It's easy to wake up and fall into our routine, but when we make the decision to seek God's presence *first*, it can change the course of our entire day.

Like any relationship, our relationship with God depends on us seeking that special one-on-one time with Him. God delights in those times of silent devotion so that He can speak into our hearts that much louder.

Jesus spent a lot of His time with the disciples, who were His close friends. He ate with them, traveled with them, and constantly talked with them about God's love. But often, Jesus retreated from the disciples and went into the wilderness alone to meditate on God's will. One of the most powerful examples of this is when Jesus prayed in the Garden of Gethsemane on the night He was arrested: "Then Jesus went with them to a place called Gethsemane, and he said to his disciples, 'Sit here, while I go over there and pray'" (Matthew 26:36, ESV). In fact, Jesus left the disciples, who were fast asleep, on three different occasions. Jesus was relentless in praying for God's help and counsel, and He repeatedly went off on His own to do so!

As you continue on your walk of faith with God, new struggles will arise; however, you don't need to be afraid. You can receive God's wisdom in everything you do—all you have to do is talk to Him. As soon as your eyes open in the morning, try to set aside distractions and spend a few minutes of silence with your heavenly Father.

NOTES

_____

_____

_____

_____

_____

_____

_____

_____

_____

GOD NOTE

"*P*lace more value on what I say about you than those around you! You will become more like me if you listen to what I say and believe me. You cannot love my Word or me and not love my creation—YOU! The voices of evil came against my Son, so don't think they will not try to accuse you as well. My Son overcame them by listening to what I had to say about Him. Listen! I say, "I LOVE YOU, AND YOU ARE PLEASING TO ME, your Father."

WEEK SIX
Rise and Shine

"Arise, shine, for your light has come, and the glory of the Lord has risen upon you."
—Isaiah 60:1 (ESV)

You may have people come into your life who try to discourage the dream God has put inside of you. When someone feels like they are drowning, they try to save themselves by pulling other people down around them. Persecution is a very real part of our Christian walk, but God assures us that He will be our light in darkness. Remember, it's not flesh and blood we're dealing with—we're dealing with Satan and his plan to keep us from our destinies!

When we experience this kind of pressure, we have to get into God's presence. Jesus told us in John 8:12, "I am the light of the world. Whoever follows me will not walk in darkness, but will have the light of life."

Think about a hot air balloon. If you want a hot air balloon to go up, you need to put more hot air in it. If you put God's truth over the opinions of the people around you, you are going to rise; those weights—regret, discouragement, and lies—have to fall off.

Don't let your circumstances weigh you down and choke out the Word— rise and shine!

It's our job to stand against the darkness so that we can raise each other up. God wants us to honor one another in love and be positive influences on the world around us. Your value is not about what you have or what you did. God says you are valuable, loved, and nothing will change the love He has for you. Let go; throw off those weights of self-pity, anger, and unforgiveness. Today is the day to stop living in the past. Drop the regrets. Rise and shine! There is a bright future ahead!

NOTES

_____

_____

_____

_____

_____

_____

_____

_____

_____

_____

"Because I am enough, you are enough—fully able to handle any challenge with your identity anchored to mine. So say not, 'I can't,' but rather, say, 'We can.'"

WEEK SEVEN

Keeping up with the Joneses

"Do not let your adorning be external—the braiding of hair and the putting on of gold jewelry, or the clothing you wear—but let your adorning be the hidden person of the heart with the imperishable beauty of a gentle and quiet spirit, which in God's sight is very precious."

—1 PETER 3:3-4 (ESV)

Did you know that roughly 15 minutes of every hour-long television show is devoted to commercials? That's a lot of advertising! If you look closely, you'll start to notice that commercials don't sell us things; they sell us an identity.

"If you drive this car, women will find you irresistible."

"If you use this insurance company, you'll be rich and powerful."

"If you wear this makeup line, you'll be as beautiful and popular as celebrities."

We have all heard the phrase "Keeping up with the Joneses," but do we realize how widespread and harmful this mind-set can be?

It's natural to take pride in your home, in your car, and even in your appearance, but the problem is when we compromise what's really important in order to find our identity in those things.

Love yourself. God does!

The enemy loves to keep us envious of others so that he can keep us ignorant of our own blessings and unique spiritual gifts. The enemy wants us to feel like we are not enough—but God tells us that we are so loved that He sent His only begotten Son to cleanse us from our sins and to help us gain admittance to His kingdom!

NOTES

_____

_____

_____

_____

_____

_____

_____

_____

_____

_____

_____

"Let me take the lead and you will find rest for your soul and more clarity in your day. As you trust me to lead you in our talks, you will see clearly the best path and will rest in peace when you must say no to the lesser path. The loud demands are a distraction, a ruse of darkness to make you miss my still, small voice, which I always reserve for those who take time with me."

WEEK EIGHT

Alone with God

"Your word is a lamp to my feet and a light to my path."
—PSALM 119:105 (ESV)

The Bible encourages us to let God's Word be our light, yet so often we forget how essential it is to read our Bible. We know we couldn't survive if we didn't eat. Yet, we allow ourselves to go days, maybe even weeks, without seeking out spiritual food. Why?

Our schedules are constantly packed with running kids to soccer practice, dance recitals, dinners, play dates, errands, and more. These things might keep us busy, but they don't keep us satisfied. Busyness can actually become a way we distract ourselves! If there are cuts to be made to the family schedule, why is it that our spiritual food is always first on the chopping block? Don't let busyness hold you back from your time with God.

So many Christians abandon the walk once they've received God's blessings. We can't let our success be our endgame.

Seek first the kingdom of God, because that is what will fill your heart and keep you satisfied. Evaluate your relationship with God. How much time are you spending with God? There are warning signs when you are spiritually malnourished; you might be having issues in your personal relationships. Once you put God back in the driver's seat, you will see a difference in your life.

Be a lover of God, not of earthly pleasures. Declutter your mind, and spend some quiet time with God. Holding on to God's Word is our lifeline! God loves you and He wants to bless you with the desires of your heart. You have purpose and potential!

NOTES

_____

_____

_____

_____

_____

_____

_____

_____

_____

_____

"**W**hen you recognize I am bringing you to a desired end, you can laugh at adversity and remain patient in the events of life, trusting that my promises will come to pass, regardless of what it feels like in the moment. Haven't I promised that this light, momentary pressure is going to result in something very rewarding and even eternal? Rejoice and laugh at the day and sometimes at yourself. It will make the burden lighter and the rejoicing even greater when you see the finish line!"

Week Nine

For Better or Worse

"Blessed is the one who perseveres under trial because, having stood the test, that person will receive the crown of life that the Lord has promised to those who love him."
—James 1:12 (NIV)

Awhile back, my husband, Gary, and I decided to do a tandem bicycle ride. I was so naive; I pictured a casual bike ride through a beautiful scenic landscape, and maybe we'd stop for a couple of picnics along the way. Oh boy, was I in for a rude awakening!

While I waited in line to register for the race, a man turned around and asked the question I was dreading: "So, how long have you been training?" I forced a smile and told him we hadn't really been training. "You're crazy!" he said. "You might as well throw in the towel right here!"

After standing in line by that man for the next 30 minutes and listening to him tell me, over and over, that we were not going to be able to finish the 100-mile ride, we set off. Quickly, I realized that it would be no easy ride. I had a choice to make: give in to defeat or pray my way to victory. When the enemy comes to steal and destroy, we need to fight back. In that moment, I made a conscious, crucial decision.

I made the choice to rejoice.

So often in our lives, we listen to those negative, doubting voices, whether they be from relatives, friends, or in our minds. The enemy wants to take us off the path God has created for us through negative voices in our lives. All of us have setbacks, but we have to stick with our purpose.

Gary and I had our setbacks during that long ride, but we made it through the 100-mile course! I knew that God did not call us to go all that way just to fail, just like God did not call you to come this far in your relationship with Him to quit when things get tough. God will reveal His picture for your life; you just have to wait on the pieces and keep pedaling.

NOTES

_____

_____

_____

_____

_____

_____

_____

_____

"Does my word define your happiness, or are you allowing my victory to be robbed by another voice? If I am your God, then why does my rule not take preeminence over them? Stop attempting to get even and instead get happy! Rejoice, for your name is written in my secret book, so it matters not whether you are in theirs."

Week Ten

Unlocking Happiness

"Take delight in the Lord, and He will give you the desires of your heart."
—Psalm 37:4 (NIV)

My mom always used to tell me, "Nobody can steal your joy unless you give them permission *first*."

I'm so thankful for those words of wisdom because she was absolutely right!

Every single day, we have two choices: we can simply react to everything happening around us, or we can take action and create the lives we want to live.

Don't give someone else the keys to your happiness!

I've known people who have everything they've ever wanted, but they're miserable. No matter what people do for them, they're always blaming *somebody* for *something*. On a bright sunny day, they find the one cloud in the sky. Then I've known people who have gone through hard situations, but they're still the happiest people I know. Nothing can steal their joy. Why? Because every person's happiness is ultimately their choice! If we put our happiness in other people's hands, we're going to be disappointed.

It's incredibly *freeing* when we take back the responsibility for how we feel. When we react to others' actions, it sets us up to be the victim. When we maintain the fact that we own our emotions, we free ourselves to be victorious in all circumstances!

Matthew 16:19 (NIV) says, "I will give you the keys of the kingdom of heaven; whatever you bind on earth will be bound in heaven, and whatever you loose on earth will be loosed in heaven."

The keys are in your hands—what are you going to do with them?

NOTES

_____

_____

_____

_____

_____

_____

_____

_____

_____

_____

"I am calling you out of the mundane, for what appears comfortable is really a mirage to keep you behind bars of apathy. I cannot allow all that has been invested in you to remain dormant. I will shake the foundations you have trusted in order to help you truly build that which is secure. There is no security apart from my will and my Word for you."

Week Eleven
Taking the First Step

"The Lord makes firm the steps of the one who delights in Him; though he may stumble, he will not fall, for the Lord upholds him with His hand."
—Psalm 37:23-24 (NIV)

Often the hardest step to take is the first one—saying yes. It's making the choice to confront your doubt and insecurities and putting everything on the line for obedience. It can be the hardest step to take, but nobody has ever walked a mile without it.

I remember many times standing on the brink of a massive breakthrough in my life and feeling scared, uncertain, and terrified to jump. Like teetering on the edge of a diving board and wondering how the water feels, that first leap in the direction God gave me felt so uncertain. Looking back on those moments now, I know there are no decisions I've made that have been more rewarding.

Unfortunately, too many people will never take that first step. God can't orchestrate your win unless you're willing to step into battle!

A couple contacted Gary and me a few years back and told us it took them getting to the end of their ropes to finally take that first step, and how saying yes changed their lives.

God had given them a business idea, but comfortable in their routine, they kept putting it on the back burner. As time went on, their financial situation grew serious. Still, they hesitated to start their business. They didn't recognize it as an answer to prayers. That first step seemed scary and risky—so they continued to put it off.

On the verge of losing everything and filing for bankruptcy, they finally took a leap of faith and started their company. Their business *took off*! Suddenly, they had cash to pay their bills, their company was thriving, and that was just the beginning! Their lives changed drastically!

They didn't have to spend years living in financial chaos; they just had to take that first step.

How many ideas has God given you that you have simply hesitated to act on? Could one of them be the answer you've believed for? Seek God for direction, and when He speaks, act! Don't wait until it's your last resort—take the first step!

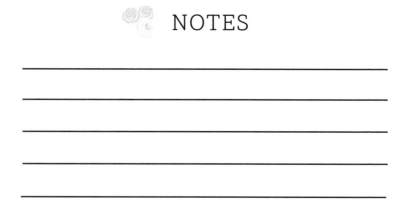 NOTES

_____

_____

_____

_____

_____

"*I* am here. There is no situation that I do not have the answer to help you manage and steer you to a victorious outcome. 'And they lived happily ever after' was my idea in the beginning. There's more to your story if you will give me the pen. Others may continuously begin this or that and repeatedly fail, but I can lead you in a sure and steady way and even turn the ups and downs into a fairytale ending as I unlock my kingdom to you. And they lived happily ever after…"

Week Twelve

Leaving Space

"He says, 'Be still, and know that I am God; I will be exalted among the nations, I will be exalted in the earth.'"

—Psalm 46:20 (NIV)

It's easy for us to get consumed with to-do lists, emails, chores, errands, and parenting, and lose sight of what God wants to do with our day. We have to learn how to leave space in our day just to stop and breathe. In Psalm 46:10, God urges us to "be still and know that I am God." Part of cultivating a healthy relationship with God is allowing time to be *still*—and not feeling guilty about it!

I constantly have to remind myself that being busy isn't my goal. In fact, the greatest ability we have is our availability! We should leave room on our calendars for creativity, spontaneity, and God's Spirit to move. When we allow space for God's Spirit to work in our day, God is able to use us in incredible ways!

When things get busy, take a second to refocus your day on God. Take a restroom break at work, a shower at home, or enjoy time with God while your children are napping. You may need to look at your schedule and let go of some things that aren't adding value to your life. However you need to do it, make it a priority to create space in your day for God to fill.

 NOTES

_____

_____

_____

_____

_____

_____

_____

_____

_____

_____

_____

_____

_____

_____

_____

_____

_____

"With the authority of my words, you must silence childhood fears and insecurities, for you are not alone or rejected. You are mine. I have called you by my name and given you an inheritance that far exceeds the pain of past experiences. Don't expect everyone will be happy for you. No matter, decide to radiate my love anyway, and refuse to let anyone extinguish the embers of my love and acceptance for you."

Week Thirteen

Goodbye, Shame

"I sought the Lord, and he answered me; he delivered me from all my fears. Those who look to him are radiant; their faces are never covered in shame."

—Psalm 34:4-5 (NIV)

"You're going to fail."

"Why even try?"

"You always mess everything up."

Have you ever let the voices of fear and shame hold you back?

I have, too many times. In fact, if you throw rejection into the mix, you're practically reading my old resume!

Many years ago, I was terrified to speak at an upcoming women's event. A woman in our church had approached me with some "encouraging" words beforehand—the kind of encouragement that's wrapped in criticism.

"I wasn't going to come since I've heard *everything* you have to say," she started, "but I decided I will so that I can give to others."

Ouch.

We made small talk for a little while longer and then ended the conversation, but one sentence kept repeating in my head: "I've heard everything you have to say."

Fear. Shame. Rejection. The alarm bells were ringing inside my head. What was I going to talk about? Had everyone heard it all before?

My confidence melted away until all I felt was a hopeless, sinking feeling.

"Who do you think you are anyway?"

"You're going to embarrass yourself in front of everyone."

Pesky, self-debilitating thoughts kept trying to steal my joy. That's when I made a decision—every time I started to have those thoughts, I was going to seek God immediately.

The day of the women's event finally came, and I climbed on that stage confidently. I delivered the message God gave me, and at the end, guess who came down to the altar in tears? The woman who said those things!

Psalm 34 promises us that those who seek God will be radiant, delivered from fear, and never covered in shame. When fear, shame, and rejection try to rise up against us, our protection is in the Word of God!

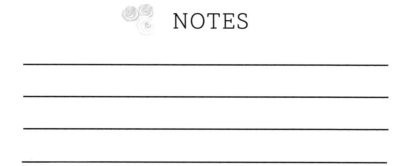 NOTES

_____

_____

_____

_____

"'The meek shall inherit the earth!' How's that for my promotion system? Don't be dissuaded by the world's system of promotion. Just when they think they have it all wrapped up, I will bust in and take from those who have stolen and falsely possessed what belongs to my beloved and give it to mine. There are those who may appear to gain, but their falsities will be seen for what they are. I promote those who walk uprightly before me, and no good thing will I withhold from them. Trust me to do it, and when tempted to bow before their idols, decide to trust me instead. In just a short bit, you will look and see the wicked no more."

Week Fourteen

Destined for More

> "'For I know the plans I have for you,' declares the Lord, 'plans to prosper you and not to harm you, plans to give you hope and a future.'"
> —Jeremiah 29:11 (NIV)

I often get asked, "What do you do when your reality doesn't look like what God promised?"

I'm reminded of a man named Joseph. Joseph was destined for great things, but that promise looked far from his reality when he found himself falsely accused and sentenced to life in prison. Joseph was born to rule Egypt, and yet he found himself in the lowest position of all—a prisoner. Still, Joseph proved his integrity when promotion seemed impossible. He held to the promise of God in the face of defeat. Long story short, overnight, Joseph ended up going from being a prisoner to ruling all of Egypt!

God turned Joseph's obstacle into his opportunity, his prison into his promotion, and his sentence into his celebration—and he can do the same for you!

You may be in the prison today, but you're not *destined* for the prison! Pass the integrity test when no one knows your name, when there's no promotion on the table, and when your situation looks hopeless, and watch how God brings His promises to pass every single time! You're destined for *more*!

 # NOTES

"*I* will teach you to love if you will allow my love to first touch your heart. You cannot give what you do not have in your possession. There is no lack in my love so much so that it is even abundantly supplied enough for an enemy. The war is not against flesh and blood, so unleash your hatred toward the real enemy, not toward people who have been controlled by heinous hatred. The force of my love is greater than any darkness and drives out fear of all kinds. When you no longer need a response because you have already received mine, you will love beyond conditions."

WEEK FIFTEEN

Without Agenda

"But love your enemies, do good to them, and lend to them without expecting to get anything back. Then your reward will be great, and you will be children of the Most High, because He is kind to the ungrateful and wicked."

—LUKE 6:35 (NIV)

We say we love a lot of things—our family, our friends, our favorite clothes, food—but what does it really mean to love like Jesus loved?

Jesus loved people unconditionally. He loved without selfish ambition. A lot of times when we say we love something, we really mean we like how something makes us feel, or what someone can do for us. Very rarely do we love with the kind of love God wants us to—without agenda.

So what does this kind of love look like?

In 1 Corinthians 13, Paul tells us that loving without agenda looks like patience. It looks like kindness. It doesn't envy, it doesn't boast, it isn't proud, it doesn't dishonor others, it isn't self-seeking, it isn't easily angered, and it doesn't keep a record of other people's wrongs. It always protects, always trusts, always hopes for the best, and always perseveres. Love isn't just how we treat people; it's how we choose to *see* people!

When we look at Paul's definition of love, how do we measure up? Are we doing a good job of loving without agenda? Every day we should strive to possess the unconditional love that Jesus demonstrated toward others. The great news is that we don't have to do it in our strength; God gave us His ability so that we could learn to love like Him!

NOTES

GOD NOTE

"I have not called you to fit in, but rather, to be a shining light in a dark place. Don't let anyone extinguish your fire. I have given you influence to make a difference. There are many voices, but do they ring true to my voice? Stay true. Mine know my voice. I do not change to make people comfortable, but my unchanging Word brings lasting comfort."

WEEK SIXTEEN
Unpopular

"What good is it for someone to gain the whole world, and yet lose or forfeit their very self?"
—LUKE 9:25 (NIV)

"How many Facebook likes did you get?"

"Are you on Instagram?"

"How many followers do you have?"

The pressure to be popular has never been greater than it is today.

We live in a media-saturated age where everyone wants to be famous, loved, and accepted—and they'll sacrifice almost anything to get there. It's easy to feel the burden to perform for social status. With a few swipes on our phones, we can easily compare our lives to our friends' through pictures and statuses. In a photoshop-obsessed culture, we have to make it our aim to be influential, not popular.

I was on a call with a marketing representative when she gave me some unexpected advice. "I don't think you should tell people you're an ex-feminist," she said. I pulled the phone a little closer, curious to hear her next words. "And I wouldn't really say you were a stay-at-home mom either. You were practically a career woman working at home. Oh, and let's not talk about being a submissive wife. You can talk about marriage, but *don't* talk about submission."

I was in shock.

Then, she added decisively, "I would stay away from politics, too. We don't want to ostracize anyone."

As we went on, I quickly realized there wasn't much I *could* talk about. Every topic seemed to be offensive to someone. I thanked her for her time and politely let her know that I couldn't compromise my message. The Bible says it's the truth that sets people free, and we are called to speak the truth in love. When we remove truth in an effort to please people, there is no freedom!

We are called to stand on the Word of God, even when it's not popular. When we endure persecution for our beliefs, we can find comfort in the fact that even Jesus, a perfect man, was criticized for speaking truth. He overcame, and so do we!

NOTES

_____

_____

_____

_____

_____

"My joy is to see you walk in the truth of my Word so that I can bless you with my kingdom now, and in future days ahead, an even greater reward as you enter into the preparations we've already made for you! Keep your eyes on my love, and your heart will continually feast on the dreams I have for you. My love created you, and my joy will sustain you until that day."

Week Seventeen

Really Happy!

"Though you have not seen him, you love him; and even though you do not see him now, you believe in him and are filled with an inexpressible and glorious joy!"
—1 Peter 1:8 (NIV)

Raising our five children was an incredible time mixed with difficult days, but also with overwhelming joy. I love happy families! Yet when I tried to think ahead to the future when my children would get married and have children, making me a grandmama, I had to strain my brain to try to grasp it, and it remained somewhat cloudy. Today they come to visit, and I hear their little feet pitter-patter across the floor as they run to find me to jump into my arms. I cannot express the sheer joy of having someone so little filled with so much love aimed at me! And then they often cry when they have to leave. My heart hurts with love for them.

That joy and intense love are like the joy we feel when we experience the knowledge of the love God has for us. And even though at times it can seem a bit cloudy with all the day-to-day tasks, it's real. There is great joy in the relationship, and we haven't yet seen Him with our natural eyes. We see Him with the eyes of our spirit. We see Him through His Word and others' encounters, but what will that day be like when we see Him face to face and fall into His arms, or maybe swoon at His feet before we can even get there?

He said, "I go to prepare a place for you so that where I am so will you be also." I prepare parties, food, presents, books to read, vacations, and activities for my children and grandchildren because I want to express my great love for them. What joy I have in the preparation! Jesus is preparing a place for us to make our joy full when we see Him. We have joy now, but we haven't seen anything yet! So if things seem a little rough today, don't forget the joy of His love and the fuller experience of that joy that is yet to come!

NOTES

"My plans for you are good, but there is a way that may seem right to this world's ideas of grandeur that leads to destruction. Are you willing to surrender the plans others have for you and your plans that are founded on illusions of success? The success I bring doesn't add sorrow to your life. It brings life and life with abundance. No longer define your identity in what others think or say, but decide to adhere to my Word and let it be the light of your purpose. My paths are peace, and although few find them, you will shine because you have!"

WEEK EIGHTEEN
Bad Habits

"Do not conform to the pattern of this world, but be transformed by the renewing of your mind. Then you will be able to test and approve what God's will is—His good, pleasing and perfect will."
—ROMANS 12:2 (NIV)

The definition of insanity is doing the same thing over and over and expecting a different result. How often do we repeat our bad habits, unhealthy choices, and wrong thought patterns, and then wonder why our lives still look like the same mess they were a month ago?

When Gary and I had just begun to pastor, I had this one woman who came to me every weekend for prayer. She was struggling with toxic emotions. Each week we'd pray, and each week she'd get free from the feelings that were tormenting her. Then the next week would come, and she would be right back where she started!

I knew there had to be more to the story.

I pulled her aside one weekend and we started to make small talk about her life. A few minutes into the conversation, she boasted proudly, "I'm going to be a porn star. That's what I'm working toward right now."

Bingo. Houston, we have a problem.

I explored the topic further, politely cautioning her and sharing God's heart on the matter. Nothing could change her mind. She was determined that's what she wanted to be, no matter what the consequences would be in her life.

You can get free every weekend, but if you're making the same unhealthy decisions during the week, your life is going to look the same. You have to change your daily habits, choices, and thought patterns if you really want to make a change in your circumstances. Your life is where it is because that's where you are. If you want your life to get better, then *you* have to get better. Learn. Develop a new skill. Try something different.

Change your habits and you can change your life!

NOTES

_____

_____

_____

_____

_____

_____

_____

_____

"My grace is sufficient to carry you through storms to your destination, but you must get in the water for my power to be made strong on your behalf. My anointing comes to those who engage my power by taking the first step. Even as in natural things a journey must begin with a step, so too my plans for you require you to walk hand in hand with me. I cannot do it for you, but I will do what you cannot do—and my grace will see you to the finish line. Begin!"

Week Nineteen

"For God has not given us a spirit of fear, but of power and of love and of a sound mind."
—2 Timothy 1:7 (NKJV)

I have done a lot of adventurous things in my life. As a mother of five, it comes with the territory. Some of those things include bungee jumping, skydiving, taking our family touring through Europe by train, and swimming with six-foot wild Lemon sharks.

I won't lie. All of those things took guts.

Now my youngest daughter is trying to convince me to go shark cage diving with her. Does it ever end? There is always something that is outside of your comfort zone, and as soon as you conquer that, it's going to be something else. So how can you be courageous enough to handle whatever comes your way? How can you be brave enough to swim with the sharks?

I promise you, you *can*. And it's easy!

If you want to swim with sharks, this is the one simple step you need to take—*jump in the water!*

Whew! That's easy, right? No?

I've discovered that many people want to know how to be free from fear, but they want an answer that removes all responsibility from them. People want to hear, "Don't worry. If you say these three words, God will take over your body and do the scary stuff for you." No matter how many times you ask the Word of God how to be courageous, you will never find *that* answer. You have a part to play, but remember, I said it would be easy! All you have to do is jump in the water, and God will take care of the sharks. You can trust God to take care of you.

When I went swimming with six-foot sharks, it only looked scary from the boat. Once I jumped into the water, it was one of the most breathtaking experiences I have ever had. I was in awe. It was the same with bungee jumping and skydiving. Once I jumped, I realized that was the hardest part, and the things I thought would be scary weren't. The hardest part is always just saying yes. When you understand that, jumping gets a lot easier!

Courage is doing something even when it *looks* scary because you know you aren't doing it alone. All you have to do is jump— say yes, step out—and God will meet you there. Don't worry about how you're going to swim with the sharks, or what comes next, just *jump*!

 NOTES

_____

_____

_____

"My Word gives you victory every time! It puts out the enemies' fire before it can take root in your heart and produce a firestorm. How much easier it is to quench or drown out a small fire. Just because a fiery dart is shot at your heart does not mean that you are destined to fail. On the contrary! I have already armed you with the water of my Word to extinguish your attackers' fire. The shield of faith goes up and the arrow is deflected. Put on my armor, my truth, my Word, and build your faith in what I say, and you will not be lacking in the day of battle."

Week Twenty

Changing Your Thoughts

"Finally, brothers and sisters, whatever is true, whatever is noble, whatever is right, whatever is pure, whatever is lovely, whatever is admirable—if anything is excellent or praiseworthy—think about such things."
—Philippians 4:8 (NIV)

Changing your thoughts and controlling your emotions are *not* easy, but both *are* possible! John 8:32 (NIV) says, "Then you will know the truth, and the truth will set you free." You can choose to put your trust in what God says about your situation instead of in your emotions.

When I was pregnant with our third child, I started showing signs of a miscarriage. It was tempting to let my thoughts and emotions run wild. I knew that if that baby was going to live, I needed to get my emotions under control. Fortunately, sometime before I had written Scriptures on index cards and put them *all over* our house. I had even stuck some on the ceiling over our bed, so as I was going to bed at night, I would see the right picture. Although I battled thoughts when my circumstances spoke contrary to the promises of God, I already had the upper hand by knowing God's truth. The preparation made me battle ready, and by staying on the truth, I won. I **gave birth to a healthy baby boy a few months later!**

If we will stay in God's Word, we are able to fight successfully. Don't wait until the evil day to prepare; instead, meditate on God's Word day and night. If an attack comes, God's Word stored up inside of you will quench it!

If you feed your spirit of fear, it's going to produce tormenting thoughts and anxiety in your life. If you feed your spirit of tragedy and hopelessness, it's going to produce feelings of depression. If you feed your spirit of faith, hope, and vision, your thoughts and feelings will line up with God's Word!

NOTES

_____

_____

_____

_____

_____

_____

_____

_____

_____

GOD NOTE

"Begin a fresh start today with me! Let go of the mental clutter of rehearsing past problems or grievances. The lighter your baggage, the farther and faster you can travel. Learn from the past, but never be confined by it. Meditate on my promises, and as you speak my Word, you build a framework for your future. My grace will give you the power to do it!"

Week Twenty-one

Creating Change

*"If any of you lacks wisdom, you should ask God, who gives generously
to all without finding fault, and it will be given to you."*
—James 1:5 (NIV)

The best day to start creating the life you want is today!

So how do you get there? How do you move from where you
are to where you want to go? These two steps are a great place
to start:

1. **Seek God's advice about your situation.**

   In addition to reading God's Word, you can pray for
   mentors, knowledge, and divine strategy on how to
   live your best life. Matthew 7:7 (NIV) says, "Ask and
   it will be given to you; seek and you will find; knock
   and the door will be opened to you." Sometimes
   getting the answers we're looking for simply starts
   with asking the questions!

2. **Implement daily practical steps.**

   If you keep doing what you did yesterday, you're
   going to keep getting yesterday's results. Seize the
   moment and commit to the changes you need to
   make to thrive! It takes time and effort, but you'll
   thank yourself three months from now.

 # NOTES

_____

_____

_____

_____

_____

_____

_____

_____

_____

_____

_____

_____

_____

_____

"*D*on't let disappointment be your guide to the future. It will always confine you to the past; instead, throw off the past and dream with me! I give a hope that doesn't disappoint. Get your hopes up and your faith in my promises activated. Even if there are twists or turns on the journey, you will arrive on the mark, and the progress will astound those watching—but you knew by faith it was coming all the while."

WEEK TWENTY-TWO

Dreams and Goals

"Write the vision and make it plain on tablets, that he may run who reads it."
—HABAKKUK 2:2B (NKJV)

Where do you want to be a *year* from now?

Habakkuk 2:2 urges us to "write the vision and make it plain." Success *always* starts with a strategy! If you can't define it, you can't obtain it. When we add clarity and deadlines to our vision, our dreams become plans and our plans become our reality. When we know what our yes is, then we know what our no has to be.

We give power to our dreams when we take the time to write them down. It's easier to prioritize our time when we have a goal in sight.

For many people, the problem isn't that they don't have goals; it's that their goals aren't specific enough to inspire action. If you want to lose weight, how much weight do you want to lose? If you want to go on a vacation, where do you want to go? If you want to transition to a new job, what would your ideal job look like?

Give yourself the freedom to dream with God and then write your future on paper!

 NOTES

_____

_____

_____

_____

_____

_____

_____

_____

_____

_____

_____

_____

_____

_____

_____

"If grace was my idea, then how do you think you can do this alone? And why do you strive to please others when I am already pleased to call you mine? You will find greater peace and more joy when you stop making comparisons to others. I made you unique, and I call you worthy of my Son's sacrifice—a great sacrifice it was. How valuable are you? Did you perform anything for that kind of love? Then why would you think my love is dependent on others' reviews, including yours? Embrace my complete love for you and be made whole."

WEEK TWENTY-THREE

Imperfect

"But He said to me, 'My grace is sufficient for you, for my power is made perfect in weakness.' Therefore I will boast all the more gladly about my weaknesses, so that Christ's power may rest on me."
—2 CORINTHIANS 12:9 (NIV)

As hard as we may try, there are *no* perfect people or relationships. We have all sinned and fallen short of the glory of God—that's not meant to condemn us but to comfort us! John 8:7 (NLT) says, "Let the one who has never sinned throw the first stone." Some people may do a better job at hiding their bad-hair days, but it's such a relief to know that it's a fact: we all have them. We can set aside our striving for perfection and be free to do our best, have fun, and learn from our missteps!

We can't thrive when we're weighed down by the expectation of perfection. And the people around us can't thrive when we put that expectation on them either. It's a weight we were never meant to carry; that's why Jesus took our inadequacies on Himself. And in their place, He left us His grace—not so that we could live a perfect life, but so that we could live a perfected life through Him.

Satan would love to make you feel isolated, like you're the only one who has bad days. Steven Furtick put it beautifully: "The reason why we struggle with insecurity is because we compare our behind the scenes with everyone else's highlight reel." Don't compare somebody's photoshopped picture with your life. If you do, you're always going to be striving toward an impossible goal. The grass is never greener on the other side; it's greener where we water it. We're going to have bad days from time to time, but the important thing is that we dust ourselves off and stay submitted to the process of refinement. Paul says that we can boast in our imperfections because they don't disqualify us from our destinies. In fact, God's ability is made perfect in our weaknesses!

NOTES

_____

_____

_____

_____

_____

_____

_____

_____

_____

_____

"If you honor me first, I will bring honor to you. If you honor people above me, then I can only leave you to the reward of their fickle ways. Flesh and blood will disappoint you, but if you want to stand strong, seek me first. Riches, honor, and long life are found in me."

Week Twenty-four

Brave Relationships

"Am I now trying to win the approval of human beings, or of God? Or am I trying to please people? If I were still trying to please people, I would not be a servant of Christ."
—Galatians 1:10 (NIV)

Being brave in relationships can be scarier than facing any feat. I should know—it took me years to learn it the hard way! The problem is, we are going to encounter people, at some point, who will try to take advantage of us. That's why we have to be courageous in our relationships; otherwise, our relationships can end up controlling us!

Here are three steps to make you bold in your relationships:

1. Focus on what is important.

Don't focus on what somebody has done to you, or said to you, but always feed everything through the filter of God's Word. Vanity says that everyone is your competition, but love says that everyone is an opportunity. Focus on who you are and what God is instructing you to do about the situation.

Psalm 29:25 (MSG) says, "The fear of human opinion disables; trusting in God protects you from that."

2. Examine the relationship.

There are times to draw a line in a relationship, and

there are times to amend an area in a relationship. People make mistakes, and it is important to choose forgiveness. However, *stay away* if a person is malicious in their intentions.

3. Don't perform for approval.

The fear of man is the fear of what others think and say about you. In other words, it is people pleasing. Performing for the approval of people is a trap from the enemy.

In the early years of our ministry, I spent way too much time trying to please people, and it hindered my ability to do what God called me to do. God couldn't trust me with His assignments when I was moved by people's opinions. If Satan can't get you to be a bully, he is going to try to get you wounded and offended by people so that he can stop you from reaching your full potential. Your identity must be secure in Christ. If you know who you are and what you have, then you know what you can do! Remember, you can change you or you can change your friends, but you can't make people change. You have to be brave and trust God!

 NOTES

_____

_____

GOD NOTE

"*I* will give you people for your life. Some will mentor you, leading you in a pathway that is solid; serve and learn from them. This is mentorship. Others will need what I have given you to help them grow; invest in them as I lead you. This is ministry. Others are tares that I did not sow at all; have nothing more to do with them and release them. This is discernment, for how can two walk together without agreement?"

Week Twenty-five

Power of Friends

"Do not be misled: Bad company corrupts good character."
—1 Corinthians 15:33 (NIV)

Friendships are *powerful.* Who we choose as friends can either hold us back or they can propel us forward.

Did you know that you become like your five closest friends? Even your income is likely to reflect theirs! Proverbs 13:20 (NIV) warns us, "Walk with the wise and become wise, for a companion of fools suffers harm." *Who* we invest our time in is just as important as *what* we invest our time into!

Inevitably, we become like the people we spend the most time with. If you want to build your *vision*, surround yourself with *visionaries.* If you've always wanted to do something specific, go out and find the person who does it the best and learn from them! Find people in your life who will challenge you to think bigger, encourage you to go further, and inspire you to keep going.

NOTES

_____

_____

_____

_____

_____

_____

_____

_____

_____

_____

_____

_____

_____

_____

_____

_____

_____

"False trust or expectations lead to a loss of joy and peace. Circumstances, the things of life, people's opinions, and performances could rob you of my simple joys and pleasures—if you misplace your affections. I loved you when you had nothing and felt as if you were nothing. How quickly the heart will chase what it esteems as valuable. Value my approval and seek me for yours. It will go better this way and you will not be left empty-handed or empty-hearted."

Week Twenty-six

Protecting Your Joy

"For the kingdom of God is not a matter of eating and drinking, but of righteousness, peace and joy in the Holy Spirit."
—Romans 14:17 (NIV)

Happiness is more than your choice; it's your *weapon*! Nehemiah 8:10b (NIV) says, "Do not grieve, for the joy of the Lord is your *strength*." It's so easy to sabotage a good day with high expectations and confused priorities, but we have to make the choice to rejoice. Here are two ways we commonly set ourselves up to lose our joy:

1. **Putting *things* first**

   Enjoying things is good and it's God's plan, but whenever we start looking to things to give us purpose, happiness, or identity, it ultimately leaves us feeling broken and empty.

2. **Putting *people's* approval first**

   Choosing the approval of people over God is a *guaranteed* formula for losing your joy. Seeking people's approval won't bring joy—it will entrap you! In fact, anything you seek more than you seek Him and His kingdom will eventually steal your happiness. Matthew 6:33 (NIV) says, "But seek first his kingdom and his righteousness, and all these things will be given to you as well." Keep your eyes on God, and your happiness will no longer be based on your circumstances!

NOTES

_____

_____

_____

_____

_____

_____

_____

_____

_____

_____

_____

GOD NOTE

"Eternity will not be made up of things you have labored over, but rather, the people. My Word and people are the only eternal investment I have placed in the earth realm. All else will fade. Let this guide your priorities and direct your choices."

WEEK TWENTY-SEVEN

The Keys to Legacy

"A good man leaves an inheritance [of moral stability and goodness] to his children's children."
—PROVERBS 13:22 (AMP)

It's so important for us to maintain an eternal perspective when we're choosing what to invest our time in. Without perspective, we waste opportunities reacting to the needs around us. What is our legacy going to be? What do we need to do *today* to build a life that leaves a lasting impact tomorrow?

Here are two keys to living a life of legacy:

1. **Distinguish between what's *good* and what's *significant*.**

   Getting the laundry done is good, but investing in the relationships around us is significant. How can we reprioritize our lives to make more time for what's significant?

   Gary's time is better spent on his work than mowing the grass twice a week. Financially, it makes more sense for us to hire someone. Don't lose track of your greatest place of effectiveness. Ask yourself, "What time-consuming responsibilities can I delegate that are pulling me away from what's significant in my life?"

2. Duplicate yourself.

Leaders don't think in terms of addition; they think in terms of multiplication. When you know how to do something well, don't do it alone. Develop a mentorship mind-set. The greatest leaders lead by coaching the people around them—including Jesus!

 NOTES

_____

_____

_____

_____

_____

_____

_____

_____

_____

_____

"Be still. Have quiet moments with me. Shhhhh! You can't hear if you can't be still. Be quiet. I lead by a still and small voice, but you will miss it if you don't stop long enough to hear it. If you want rest for your soul, then unplug for a moment from the forces that control you. Quantity does not always produce quality, but it does make room for it. How much time have you given me? I do not work on your schedule. Come seek mine and watch yours abound! It's not that I am not there in the busyness; it's just that you won't recognize me."

WEEK TWENTY-EIGHT

Uninterrupted

"My dear brothers and sisters, take note of this: Everyone should be quick to listen, slow to speak and slow to become angry."
—JAMES 1:19 (NIV)

Uninterrupted. Has that word been lost in a culture of cell phones and technology? How many uninterrupted moments do we really get every day?

At dinner, our phones silently let us know they're there, lighting up with notifications, tempting us to sneak a peek. I'm always startled when I go out to dinner and find tables full of families, each with a phone in their hand engaged in conversations with a million different people but the ones sitting right in front of them.

It's no wonder that although the younger generation is in constant contact with each other, they're the loneliest.

We have to be intentional about finding quality time with the people we love. Quality time means no interruptions. It means shutting off your phone and giving someone your undivided attention. It means going beyond being *present* and choosing to be *engaged* in the lives around you.

Sometimes we stumble upon quality time in the middle of quantity time, but if we aren't looking for opportunities to engage with the people around us, we can have all the time in the world with somebody and still never connect. A good friend once told me that quality time starts when we stop to *listen,* and she was absolutely right!

Are you looking for opportunities to listen to the people around you with the intention of *understanding* them better? We have to be intentional about shutting off distractions and living in the moment by engaging with the people around us. Shut off the distractions and meet the people you love all over again—uninterrupted.

NOTES

_____

_____

_____

_____

_____

_____

_____

_____

_____

"Come away and let me refresh you with my presence, and you will have a merry heart, a feast that cannot be diminished, amply supplied. You will ride on the high places with me, and I will show you my secrets. Can there be a greater place to escape? No need for money or vacation time, just you and me and the delights of my perspective. Love. Life. Joy. My goodness. Inner acceptance and love for me, yourself, and others awaits."

Week Twenty-nine

Unplugged

"Come to me, all you who are weary and burdened, and I will give you rest."
—Matthew 11:28 (NIV)

We have to learn to be still and know God, or there is no time to *dream* dreams, *think* of how to create them, and *be present* in the moment. We need perspective! It refreshes our spirits, souls, and bodies when we rest in God's presence. It's always hard for me to put the to-do list aside and listen, but it's so rewarding!

One of the biggest keys to keeping your joy is to establish and protect your day off every single week. No "quick" email breaks, business calls, or meetings—as hard as that may sound. God *created* you for a day of rest.

When Satan realized he couldn't tempt Jesus, the Bible says he left him to wait for an opportune time. Satan is always looking for an opportunity to tempt us—and he usually strikes when we're worn out. When we don't take time to rest, we set ourselves up for temptation!

Often the biggest areas where we miss it are the easiest and simplest ones to do. That's because we expect them to fall into place naturally, but practicing the habit of rest every week takes effort. We have to be *intentional* about unplugging from the stress of our day-to-day and finding rest in God's presence.

Practice self-love and you'll reap the benefits of a happier, healthier you, as well as happier, healthier relationships!

NOTES

_____

_____

_____

_____

_____

_____

_____

_____

_____

_____

_____

_____

_____

GOD NOTE

"*I* have written you on the palm of my hands! You could never be forgotten. Though you may feel this way, it's not true to my nature. I paid a high price because I love you! My love is not fickle and it does not change. I have counted and numbered your hairs as well as your days. You are in my book. In me, you live. In me, you move. In me, you have your very being. Your value is established, and your worth is clearly defined by my actions."

WEEK THIRTY

You're Not Forgotten

"If I rise with the sun in the east and settle in the west beyond the sea,
even there you would guide me. With your right hand you
would hold me."
—PSALM 139:9-10 (NCV)

When Gary and I were in the midst of financial chaos and living in an old farmhouse, there were days I felt like God must have forgotten about me. My life did *not* look the way I had envisioned—I was voted "most likely to succeed" in high school. Now I found myself trimming the plants growing through our broken window frames!

I couldn't see the incredible plan God was unraveling in my life. Looking back, the beautiful work God was doing is crystal clear. God knew our names, even in that old farmhouse, and He was guiding us every step of the way. God had a plan, and it was so much better than anything I ever could have imagined!

God hasn't forgotten about you. He knows where you are, He knows where you're going, and He knows how to get you there. God knows your name. Whatever you're facing today, give your emotions over to God, and allow Him to work in the situation. You don't have to do life alone. God has gone before you, is with you, and has already made a way for you.

NOTES

_____

_____

_____

_____

_____

_____

_____

_____

_____

_____

_____

_____

_____

_____

_____

_____

_____

"It is a work of the flesh to cover sins, shortcomings, and insecurities, but it is the work of my Spirit to reveal them so that you can mature into the beautiful creation I made you to be. Do you want to grow and truly be or simply try to pretend? Let go of the cocoon, embrace the truth, and be set free for the flight of your life!"

WEEK THIRTY-ONE

Renovated

"For I am about to do something new. See, I have already begun! Do you not see it? I will make a pathway through the wilderness. I will create rivers in the dry wasteland."
—ISAIAH 43:19 (NLT)

I love fixing things! It's part of my DNA. But sometimes, it's me that needs fixing. Recently, I renovated a holiday home that had been in our family for 33 years. In doing so, I had the opportunity to evaluate myself. I realized the changes I had to make in myself were a lot like the ones I had to make in the home. As I sorted through the house's contents, there were items that, after 33 years, needed to be discarded. Others could be repurposed with a fresh coat of paint or a new location. I had combed through magazines and the Internet to purchase items to breathe new life and an updated feel to the home. Yet, other items were just perfect as they were, some even priceless with memories attached. Among the priceless items was a mural of a nautical seascape my mother painted many years ago.

As I sorted, I asked myself questions such as, "Is this special?" "Do I like it?" "Is it a distraction or a focal point?" "Does it add to or take away from my room (life)?" "Is it useful, or is it taking up space where something else should belong?"

The same holds true in our lives. God is doing a work in all of us. Some things are tattered and worn out—our excuses, our grudges, guilt, pride, and shame. We need to let go and discard these things or they clutter our lives. Some gifts and talents we possess need to be repurposed for God's glory instead of ours. Priceless treasures are not always being appreciated the way they should because we need to sort and remove what really doesn't matter to locate what does. There must be new life breathed into our lives—new learnings, open hearts, and clear calendars to write new chapters in our life stories. I did a lot of thinking while I tore out old carpet, painted, laid tile, and decorated utilizing the old and new. After much work, I was pleased with the outcome.

The Holy Spirit wants to point out some areas where we need to let Him clear debris from the past that is not profitable to us or others. We need a fresh perspective on our lives and to see ourselves honestly so that we can let Him do the renovations. He cannot if we will not. If we will cooperate and allow Him to do the work, we will see amazing progress, and the real hidden treasures will come forth as the focal points of our house. We need to ask ourselves the tough questions. If we don't ask, who will? Let's do some honest, soul-searching, house-decluttering work, and emerge new people.

 NOTES

"Well done, my good and faithful servant! You may not see the reward of everything you've sown yet, but the harvest is coming. Your labor and obedience have not been in vain. I have called you for a purpose and I am pleased with your heart for me!"

Week Thirty-two

Thank You

"Then we will no longer be infants, tossed back and forth by the waves, and blown here and there by every wind of teaching and by the cunning and craftiness of people in their deceitful scheming."
—Ephesians 4:14 (NIV)

I received a text with a bold phrase from one of my children that read, "Thank you, Mom, for disciplining us!" My child is 33 years old (interestingly, the age Jesus started His ministry), and now the thank-you comes for work done many, many years before. This is true of valuable investments in all areas. It's not always the short or quick gratifications but the more lasting ones that take the longest time to cultivate. But we want quick results! That's one of the reasons we must stay committed to doing things according to God's design in His Word. Fads come and go, and the culture grabs on to them like a lifeline, but time-tested results won't be found in trends. It takes a real foundation of truth to build lasting success.

I later learned that my child was witnessing the effects of what parental discipline being neglected had done in another's life—and was grateful that was not their life! When someone understands the fear of the Lord (or we could say respect for God's authority), along with it comes wisdom and understanding. Without these, a person's life is riddled with problems, and they lack the disciplines that bring the fruit of God's Spirit or successful lives. It is the child whom God approves whom He corrects. We can have it our way or we can have it His way. Children left to themselves bring shame to their parents according to Proverbs. Aren't you glad God loves you and me enough to discipline us so that we can live, so that we can be freed from the self-centered pursuits of doing things our way instead of His? It's not in our best interest to always get things our way. A peaceful life doesn't come from demands we make but from steps we take toward maturity.

NOTES

"*T*rust my heart for you and my ability to bring you into the destiny created for you. As you trust that my hand is strong on your behalf, you will be less likely to be wounded or moved by the voice of others. I am trustworthy, a friend who sticks close when you feel left out or alone. I will never leave you and my good plans for you are not controlled by another."

WEEK THIRTY-THREE

Mending Hurt Feelings

"Bear with each other and forgive one another if any of you has a grievance against someone. Forgive as the Lord forgave you."
—COLOSSIANS 3:13

Hurt feelings destroy so many relationships. We all do and say things that often unintentionally hurt another. And in the course of life and relationships, our own feelings get hurt. Most of these slights and misunderstandings are just that, misunderstandings. There is the occasional intentional offensive action, but much of the time it's unintentional. While we can't change this in others, we can work on our relationships and especially ourselves.

After years of working with people and observing my own shortcomings, I've come to the conclusion that our egos (or may I say our *pride*) get in the way of relationships. We're all looking for others to make us feel special, valued, and even exceptional; and when others fail to do what we need, we get our feelings hurt. We retreat, or sulk, or punish the other person with our withdrawal. I've watched friendships be destroyed, marriages broken, families devastated, businesses fail, and, worse, God's kingdom hindered, because we bruise easily and our pride keeps us from mending the hurts.

The enemy is looking for an open door in all of our lives. Getting our feelings hurt and harboring an offense over it is the number-one way I know he enters lives—next to blatant disobedience or rebellion.

What should we do when we get hurt? First, pray. Pray and ask God to help you sort through your hurt. Hurt usually leads to offense, then anger, and then paybacks through disloyalty and betrayal. At which phase of the pathway are you? God always helps us see things through His eyes. It minimizes the offense and helps us see our lack of innocence in the situation.

I once saw a Facebook post where a Christian was calling out another Christian for saying some offensive things and for judging a situation unfairly and being insensitive. Of course, people began to pile on the offenses, insults, and judgments and suggesting paybacks to justify their friend's hurt. It was clear that they were all guilty of the very thing that they had accused the other person of in the first place.

Prayer helps us see things as they are, not as we justify ourselves to "feel." *It's much easier to forgive others when we realize just how much forgiveness we need.* Pray and then choose to forgive just as God chose to forgive us through Jesus.

Forgiveness is different from compromise. We cannot compromise what God says about a subject in order to "love" someone. We love the person, and we can embrace a person but not embrace sin as acceptable. But first, we must get the plank out of our own eye.

Once we choose to forgive by faith in the work of Jesus, now we have a right mind and heart toward the other person. If we need to talk this situation out, then the Holy Spirit will show us how to go about it in a spirit of love and will also show us the right timing.

There are situations that are better left unspoken—when we have harbored something in our heart, we can deal with God alone. Then there are times we must go and talk through situations with others in a true spirit of humility and desire for reconciliation. We must hear how and when to do this from the Holy Spirit. Regardless of how other people may get offended or react in life, we can stay free from offense when we honor God and the people He made and loves. The Golden rule to "do unto others the way you would want them to do unto you" is *still* golden.

Next time you are hurt, don't take to Facebook. Instead, take the following three simple steps:

1. Pray.
2. Forgive.
3. Develop a plan of communication and restoration.

NOTES

"My good, pleasing and perfect will is always available to you in the moment you feel least capable to follow it. By my Spirit I make a way of escape if you will cry out for my help. There is escape from the dictator, the flesh, that has always demanded you follow its ways and appetites. Your spirit is willing but the flesh is weak; don't let it control you. We both can't lead, so let my Spirit rule and reign in your heart—and in your emotions."

WEEK THIRTY-FOUR

Soul Sister

"*May God himself, the God of peace, sanctify you through and through. May your whole spirit, soul and body be kept blameless at the coming of our Lord Jesus Christ.*"
—1 THESSALONIANS 5:23 (NIV)

Don't let your soul be in control! We can live out of our spirit and give God the reins to our life or we can let our soul (mind, will and emotions) dictate our life. Even though God gave us these faculties, He didn't intend for our physical senses or the soul to lead and direct our lives, since they can be so easily lead astray. The world, the flesh and the enemy can manipulate and influence all these areas. The only sure way to know what is right is to be led by the Spirit—or, as the scripture says, to "walk in the Spirit."

God gave us a soul, but the only way to live blameless is to let our soul and body be sanctified or separated unto God by giving the Spirit of God control. He wants to lead us by the Spirit. If we choose to submit our mind, will and emotions to God, we will not be misdirected by logical deductions or fickle feelings. We can know what the will of God is and allow our feelings, thoughts, will and senses to be directed by His truth. We will be preserved or kept free from harmful consequences and live in His righteousness through Jesus Christ our Lord.

Are you allowing the Spirit to separate your feelings from what faith in God's Word instructs you to believe and act on?

NOTES

_____

_____

_____

_____

_____

_____

_____

_____

_____

_____

_____

_____

"See what I see: my unrelenting commitment to their best, gift-wrapped in forgiveness; that's how I see—commitment to believe the potential, to see the finish from the start, truthfulness to remove falsehood, forgiveness erasing the past, making room for the present."

WEEK THIRTY-FIVE

Say Yes to Friendships

"God settles the solitary in a home; he leads out the prisoners to prosperity, but the rebellious dwell in a parched land."
—PSALM 68:6 (ESV)

When we come into God's kingdom, we come into a family, the family of God. This transformation should impact every relationship in our lives! We must learn how to walk in the grace or empowerment that is ours in our marriage, family, home, friendship and life. Gary and I have raised five godly children who serve the Lord. I understand the vulnerabilities in relationships, potential problems and the stress of caring for others, but you can have success and fulfillment in this area!

God has answers for our connections to people. Ultimately, our greatest joys (and potential sorrows) come from relationships with those we love, so we need to learn how to invest into them God's way and free ourselves from wrongful expectations and hurtful words and actions. There is an anointing from God to enjoy relationships, and you can have tremendous joy as you are empowered to be the friend, wife, husband, father, mother and minister that God has called you to be.

All relationships must be built on trust, unconditional love (acceptance), an exchange of giving, receiving and forgiveness. It is completely unrealistic to think that any one of us is going to always get it right or that others will not fail at times in these areas. We are dying to selfishness, the demand to get our own way, what we want when we want it. Sometimes the flesh doesn't let go of its desire to be in control easily.

Relationships are God's way to teach us more about His love and us. I have learned more about the depths of God's love while attempting to love my family. The only way to be successful in relationships is to learn how He does it!

NOTES

_____

_____

_____

_____

_____

_____

_____

_____

_____

_____

"I have loved you with an everlasting love. Let all purpose and pursuits you seek flow from this revelation. It will heighten your sense of what is purposeful today."

Week Thirty-six

Purposed

> "*Making the most of every opportunity, because the days are evil.*"
> —Ephesians 5:16 (NIV)

You can't give out of an empty vessel. Value others *and yourself* because God does. So, how can you best invest your time and energy? Here are some ideas on how to do so wisely:

Don't overcommit. Yes, it is possible, in an attempt to please God and others, to overcommit or to be taken advantage of in relationships, and even sometimes in Christian service. I've been there myself. I think it's important to learn how to hear God's direction in making long-term commitments, especially when a large amount of time commitment or financial assistance is required. But doesn't God want us to meet every need? Interestingly enough, even Jesus differentiated between the demands that were placed on Him. It was people's faith that connected them to the answers He had for them, not His own. Later, the disciples turned down a request for finances but met the need in a different way—*God's way*. They said, "Silver and gold have I none, but such as I have I give."

Evaluate relationships. I've learned that there are people who are consistently takers and there are those who instead look to give. We all have times of need, so as we have freely received we also should give to others. Healthy relationships should have times of giving and receiving to be solid. Even mission work and serving the poor need to be balanced by seeking God for the best method to help. We must determine God's answer to meet the need. Otherwise, we keep others who need to step up from doing so if we consistently take false responsibility to fix their problems. It can also be unhealthy if our identity or motivation is found in our works.

When we work to obtain love, we will always feel shorted. This can manifest in resentment, as commitments to friends, job demands and relationships with takers leave us empty. We can even do too much to meet our children's demands, without expecting them in turn to contribute at their level of age and ability. Consistently working 60 hours each week at our job or constantly cleaning up after our 13-year-old may make us feel needed, but it will bankrupt us spiritually, physically and emotionally, and will hurt others' ability to grow and take personal responsibility. Everyone needs accountability so that they can become their very best. Real love holds others accountable.

Identify with God's love for you and others. You are loved, accepted and pleasing to God; and if you're content in that, any giving you do for others should come from your identity solidly rooted in Christ. That said, one of the greatest blessings in life is to give, and it truly is more blessed to give than to receive. Not only does God reward us, but we can also find a deep satisfaction in knowing that He led us to do so. If you give out of obligation or necessity, then it can be a drain, and it can wear you down and create resentment. Let your giving be done out of security in your identity in Him, and let it be by His Spirit, and of course done with joy! God loves it when we give cheerfully.

Let your giving be motivated by love. *This is my commandment: that you love one another that your joy may be full.* Joy is an inner force that comes from God's Spirit. It emanates out of receiving love—*real love* from God—and then giving it away to others. As we love Him first, He will teach us how to love others (and love ourselves) from His vantage point. Only good things come from seeing ourselves, our relationships and others the way God does. As we do, we can give to others from what we have. Loving others brings joy! But living to please others, or giving to gain acceptance, love, personal gain or approval, makes giving turn into a weight. Instead, we must live in the freedom of giving from God's river of love.

Forgive quickly. But what about those who have hurt us? Love doesn't keep a record of that. It just keeps loving because of the overflow of love from God. Someone's deficit of love can't rob me of my love reservoir if I have an overflowing source from God. Now, that doesn't mean I don't hold them accountable for their decisions or apply consequences when necessary, but I don't have to become bitter if they choose to wrong me in some way. I actually feel badly for them, because I know they will reap what they have sown.

Prioritize. Every demand doesn't have the same priority. We need to pray and ask God to help us honor Him first, then our spouse, our children, our provision or vocation, and then our ministry to family, friendships and others. For each of us to be our best, we must care for ourselves, too!

NOTES

"It may appear that you have lost when you release something into my hand, but I have not forgotten. I am the promise keeper and I will return your gift with larger measure and a greater portion. Once my hand has touched it, multiplying grace changes it into a new harvest that will come back in many days, in greater ways!"

Week Thirty-seven

Promises to Prosper

"And everyone who has left houses or brothers or sisters or father or mother or wife or children or lands for My name's sake, shall receive a hundredfold and will inherit eternal life."

—MATTHEW 19:29

We were trying to sell our house during the oil crisis in Tulsa, but so many houses were on the market. My husband had come in from jogging many months before and said, "We are moving." I said, "I know, but where?" "Columbus, Ohio. God spoke to me." Our house had been on the market with no nibbles for six months, and we were now several house payments behind. Worse yet, we were upside down on the mortgage since the economy had sunk.

We went to the banker and asked what to do. She said, "We will allow you to sell it for what it appraises for, but good luck finding a buyer." I can remember one Sunday morning hearing an evangelist share Matthew 19 about leaving houses for God's kingdom. We had both already left our families to go to Bible school in Tulsa, but now I realized that I needed to give this house to God and claim His promise to sell it. I prayed in faith and declared it "sold, in the name of Jesus." God gave me a creative idea to list the house that weekend and do my own open house. We had been released from our realty contract, so I could now do the selling partnered with God.

That weekend he brought a buyer who had a deal fall through earlier in the week. She was a believer who had a list of what she prayed for in a house. She had tried to buy the other one in a compromise, and when it fell through she trusted God. Our house met her every desire. God blessed us both! Many years later, God would bring back this promise and bless us with an amazing dream home in Ohio.

Anything given up to God is never lost. It simply returns with a greater blessing at a later time!

NOTES

_____

_____

_____

_____

_____

_____

_____

_____

_____

"*I* have called you to bring forth fruit. Don't forget that fruit comes as you cultivate the seed. The seed of my Word planted in your heart, watered and kept alive must bring a harvest. It cannot fail. Cultivate, water, repeat and grow. It's time to mature in what you know. Close the gap between your knowing and growing into obedient fruitfulness."

Week Thirty-eight
Press On

> "*I press toward the goal for the prize of the upward call of God in Christ Jesus. Therefore, let us, as many as are mature, have this mind.*"
> —Philippians 3:14-15b

Pressure applied in the right direction creates positive change. If you don't like the direction your life is going, then begin to put pressure in the right direction. Get ahold of God's principles and press them into your head, your heart and your lifestyle. I promise they will create change. Sometimes we are tempted to think that the Word of God is not changing things or that we aren't changing fast enough, but if you look back at how far you have come, you are being transformed. You aren't the same as you used to be, and if you keep exerting force against darkness, you will drive it far from your life.

Maintaining never works, because we live in an evil, earth-cursed world. Just about the time you think you are maintaining, you realize you are slipping back. God calls you and me to advance. Move forward, even if it seems like a glacial pace. Sometimes slow growth is more permanent growth. Just as glaciers can slowly move through an area and cut a permanent valley, so too you can make a permanent difference in your life and your family's heritage by pressing forward with God's Word!

 NOTES

GOD NOTE

"You say, 'I don't know how to do this! I feel overwhelmed!' You only have to ask me for the wisdom, assistance and guidance you seek. You don't have to attempt it alone. I have created you for relationship. Let me be the sounding board and the friend you seek. I ordered the universe and I know how to help you manage your tasks. I'll send others, but first things first. Start with me and let my Spirit direct your steps and bring alignment in your life. Light be and order come!"

Week Thirty-nine

Simplify

"*For though I am far away from you, my heart is with you. And I rejoice that you are living as you should and that your faith in Christ is strong.*"
—Colossians 2:5 (NLT)

Order is a powerful way to advance your life. Busyness is not necessarily the same as advancement. We can be busy working at the wrong things (like watching too much TV), but it's not going to advance our lives. Not only do we need to choose the highest priorities, but we also need to be productive at bringing order to those areas.

When Adam and Eve sinned, disorder and chaos came into the world, and everyone born into sin was born with a natural tendency to buck order. You know what I am talking about–the tendency to overeat, to leave a mess behind, to be slothful in business, to allow the weeds to take over!

We don't need to buck God's order; we need to buck the world's system of calling evil good and good evil, which produces chaos in life. Order comes through discipline. I know that's not a popular word, but discipline is the road to freedom!

If we are disciplined in our finances today, we will have more opportunities tomorrow. If we put it away now, our house will be easier to keep clean. If we have the discipline to make the tougher choices today, we can celebrate victories tomorrow. Many people want the success they have seen Gary and me have, but they are unwilling to do what we did to get there. Yet, we are still making decisions today to discipline ourselves so that tomorrow will be more fruitful.

Organize your life. Clean your house. Simplify your lifestyle so that you can maintain it with order. Properly align your relationships, finances and family. Order will bring blessing!

NOTES

_____

_____

_____

_____

_____

_____

_____

_____

_____

"*I* see the beginning from the end and it is a good end, to bless you beyond this present hardship. Do not quit when pressure is great for there is no dream without labor, no baby without birth, and there is no sweetness in victory without a fight. What I am forming in you is greater than the resistance, so stay the course! See by faith the finish line."

WEEK FORTY

Living on Purpose

"'For I know the plans I have for you,' declares the Lord, 'plans to prosper you and not to harm you, plans to give you hope and a future.'"
—JEREMIAH 29:11 (NIV)

We are purposed to live our life in victory and finish our race strong in the Lord. How we finish is just as important, if not more so, as how we start. It is important to build on the right foundation, but starting doesn't get us to the prize alone—we must finish strong! And we must discover why we are here.

For such a time as this you were born! You are purposed to be light in the darkness, to demonstrate God's kingdom. It doesn't surprise God that you are living in this time. He planned it before the foundations of the world. Too many of us live lives without living on purpose.

I searched for years trying to figure out what, in addition to my family, was my purpose? What was my passion? I looked for clues in everything, from things I enjoy to things that get me angry—such as injustices against children and young women. I also looked at places in which I have volunteered to figure out what matters most to me. I came to the conclusion that, even before we started to pastor a church, I loved motivating people in our company meetings to do their best and succeed financially. I love encouraging people so that they can live lives of freedom, enjoy their families, and fulfill their destinies in God. I realized my calling wasn't so much to a specific age group or gender, but rather to all people, helping them rise to their destiny and reach their potential.

My good friend Patty said, "If there is a little shampoo left in the bottle, you don't want to throw it out, because you want to see it accomplish what it was made for." I had to laugh. She's right. I want everything to fulfill its purpose—after all, even my shampoo was made for a purpose. I am passionate about people winning in life, because that's the way God created and designed them to live. (I have since let go of almost-empty shampoo bottles for higher goals.)

Destiny is one of the reasons I am passionately against excuses and blame, because I know that a person can never move forward if they blame someone else for where they are today. We have all been hurt. We have all seen sorrows and tough times. But if you can find one example in life or in the Word of God of someone who overcame, then you can too! This is not a lack of compassion; it's the knowledge that compassion must move us to action! Belief in God and His Word mixed with positive action is the answer. *God's kingdom principles don't change—but they do change things.*

Our life was completely rerouted and changed as we continually stuck with the hard stuff when we wanted to quit many times.

But don't quit. There is only one *you*, and only you can accomplish the call God placed on your life. If you don't, then who will?

NOTES

"*I* am the cord that unites. A rope of two unravels easily yet is stronger when twined with three. As you become intertwined with me, you find unbreakable unity of my purpose. This cannot be achieved apart from me nor by selfish ambition or lopsided pursuits. Seek my true purpose for you as one and run with the same destination in focus, multiplying your unending love and satisfying accomplishments."

Week Forty-one

Guard Your Marriage

"And the two shall become one flesh."
—Ephesians 5:31b

My husband and I have spent thirty years working as a team. If a husband and wife are to be one, then their goals, effort and majority of their time need to focus toward a common vision. I have observed marriages where each spouse is pursuing a different destination, going after their own mission, hobbies and success stories. Oftentimes one of them ends up successful at their individual career, but the marriage doesn't meet with success.

In the creation of woman, God says it isn't good for a man to be alone. And when He makes Eve for Adam, He calls woman a helpmeet, one who helps meet the need that a man has for a companion, wise counselor, encourager and partner in life. Our modern world of independence shuns the idea of this picture of two people who are interdependent on each other. If we are truly one, then how do you separate a husband and wife and send them in two directions and expect them to grow as one? Ultimately, you hear the verdict of this lifestyle: "We just grew apart and went our separate ways." Unfortunately, the culture thinks that this is one—"Every man or woman for himself." Yet, this attitude misses the greatest joy of growing old together and sharing life's journey with the same best friend—one's spouse.

Guard your marriage and don't break faith with the wife of your youth, husbands. Wives, respect and honor your husband. Spend time together pursuing a common vision. God brought you together not to live and pursue separate lifestyles but to be co-heirs in this life. I discourage dual careers that take two people in opposite directions. If you both must work at separate careers, make sure it's for a common goal and vision, and that there is a tremendous amount of time spent cultivating and exchanging ideas, dreams and plans!

NOTES

_____

_____

_____

_____

_____

_____

_____

_____

_____

"Get up! Stand up and dust off the dirt, the distractions to your dream. The dream still remains there just underneath the surface dirt of the day. My Word can wash off the debris and reveal it afresh! Polish it up and see your reflection in me."

WEEK FORTY-TWO

Dreams

"Faithful is He who calls you, and He also will bring it to pass."
—1 THESSALONIANS 5:24 (NAS)

My dreams as a little girl were to be a teacher, a news anchor, and a world traveler as an ambassador to nations. Many of the influences around me encouraged me to reject ideas of marriage and having children. After I was born again, I struggled between what was right according to God and what the world said was right. I needed to know what God wanted for my life. He began to speak dreams and whisper small steps to the pathway into my heart. It seemed like these dreams and visions would never happen. I took the steps I felt He was giving me, but there were times, I must confess, along the journey that it looked like a pipe dream.

What about you? Have you ever struggled with feeling like you couldn't do it God's way because it takes too long or you don't believe it's working? Or you think you won't measure up to God's standard to get it His way, so you do it your way instead? Have you ever had the thought that if you were going to make it, you couldn't do it as a Christian, because the world shuts out opportunities unless we compromise?

This isn't true! I have had all these thoughts, failings and many setbacks, but God's promises to me have come to pass. Even my dreams as a little girl have come to pass—I teach God's

Word, I anchor TV programs, and I travel as an ambassador for Christ. I can promise that if you will do the best you can to keep getting back up and pursuing God, then He will bring to pass that which He promised!

NOTES

_____

_____

_____

_____

_____

_____

_____

_____

_____

_____

_____

"Joy is the outcome of your faith, your agreement with my Word. By faith you see and agree, by joy you agree and react in strength when it looks impossible. Choose to react with joy to the pressures, the pains, the problems and watch me create a feast for you in the presence of opposition. Sing, make a joyful sound of praise! You are blessed and nothing can stop my Word or power when you choose joy!"

Week Forty-three

Contagious Joy

"May the God of hope fill you with all joy and peace as you trust in him."
—Romans 15:13a (NIV)

There is a connection between what you believe and your joy! Choose to believe what God and His Word say to you and about you. Meditating on your failures, mistakes and what someone did or said will make you negative and zap the strength out of you. What you meditate on becomes a belief. Therefore, you must guard yourself from wrong thinking and wrong believing.

Think happy thoughts! Sing happy songs! Hum a tune. Do something positive. Create. Do things that inspire you to be your best. Laugh. Spend time in God's Word and worship Him in joy and freedom. Life is in Christ! Out of a personal relationship with God, you can believe good things about who you are in Him, and you can rejoice!

It takes effort to make yourself believe good things when others are negative, but you will have what you believe. I remember going to hear one of my favorite female ministers, and she gently rebuked the women at a ministers' wives' luncheon. She said something like, "Don't look at me like that with your judgmental attitudes. I know what you think, but you get what you believe, and I get what I believe." I have never forgotten it, because as I grew in ministry opportunities I began to see the attitude to which she referred and to hear the negative words and criticisms toward those who believe and teach faith.

Don't let the enemy steal your joy with regrets, dread of what you have to do, legalism, ruts, worry, anxiety, mental reasoning, negativity, manipulative people, unbelief or overcommitments! Believe what God says, and serve the Lord with gladness. He is better than anything anyone can do or say against Him!

Joy is contagious! People should see you smile and know that there is something different about you! This hope you have in Him will not leave you disappointed! Get your happy on!

NOTES

_____

_____

_____

_____

_____

_____

_____

_____

GOD NOTE

"I have loved you simply for you. Rest in that love and respond with your love for me by your obedience to my Word. It brings life. My love for you is not dependent on your performance, but I delight in your loving response, for if you love me you will obey me."

Week Forty-four
Peace Over Performance

"Finally, brothers and sisters, rejoice! Strive for full restoration, encourage one another, be of one mind, live in peace. And the God of love and peace will be with you."
—2 Corinthians 13:11

Struggling to perform in a way we think will make others happy keeps us in a constant state of confusion, turmoil, and insecurity, instead of peace. When my oldest daughter had her first birthday, I put hours into making a beautiful, themed cake. It was such a success that a friend attending the party asked if I could make one for her daughter's birthday, too.

"Of course!" I said eagerly, proud that my cake had turned out so nicely that she wanted an encore.

When her daughter's birthday came two weeks later, I cheerfully pulled out my cooking supplies and got to work on her daughter's cake. That's when something went terribly wrong. While baking, the cake mounded high in the center, and then it exploded like a volcano! Hours away from the party, what's a girl to do? I gave her my word. I didn't want to fail. With no time to bake another cake, and my pride stopping me from running to the store and buying one—I tried to fix my sad mess of a cake. It was hopeless. Finally I sat down in the kitchen floor, leaned up against the cabinets, and cried. I felt like a failure. Surely she would no longer want me as a friend!

My entire self-worth and value were tied to baking a cake, of all things!

I must have looked ridiculous when my husband walked in and found me crying on the floor beside my destroyed cake. After I explained the situation, he said reassuringly, "It's just a cake; it's not the end of the world. It doesn't look that bad."

With his encouragement, in one last attempt, I quickly decorated the "volcano" with plastic bear figurines and hurried to the party, puffy-eyed and late. When my friend opened the door, I began apologizing over and over for my disastrous result of a cake. She took one look at the cake and began laughing—and laughing—and suddenly I was laughing, too. I quickly realized how silly I was being. It was a cake for a one-year-old! The more we looked at the flowing-volcano, dancing-bear cake, the more we laughed. My friend loved it, and I learned to laugh at myself and rest in the comfort that even when things go wrong, I am still loved. View life with the mind of Christ—understand you are complete in His love; the less you base that love on your performance, the greater your peace becomes.

NOTES

_____

_____

_____

_____

GOD NOTE

"My forgiveness has freed you to forgive others and be a messenger of deliverance to many who are lost in a mental and emotional quagmire of pain. Never forget this great salvation and extend it to others by releasing them and yourself from the prison of the past with its failures and shortcomings. I set you free, so free others!"

WEEK FORTY-FIVE

Forgiven

"If it is possible, as far as it depends on you, live at peace with everyone."
—ROMANS 12:18

How do you deal with pressure without losing your patience?

I can't say that I have always gotten an "A" on my report card, but I have learned quite a few lessons the hard way. When our children were smaller and we were struggling financially in the old farmhouse, the pressure caused a lot of tension in our marriage. I remember one morning Gary and I had a disagreement about something, and I went huffing and puffing in anger up the stairs to our bedroom. It's funny looking back; I don't even remember what it was about. I was pregnant during the time, which certainly didn't help!

Shortly after, our 6-year-old daughter came trotting through the door. She unfortunately had witnessed the whole scene play out. I sat up in bed to greet her, and she said in her sweet little voice, "Mommy, are you going to forgive Daddy?"

I thought, *Not that! Why did she ask that?*

I softened somewhat and replied, "In a little bit, sweetheart."

She held up a Bible she had carried upstairs with her and handed it to me. "I think you need to read this," she said. Then, she turned around and disappeared to play. Talk about conviction!

I tried to rationalize putting off forgiving him, but she was right. God had forgiven me too many times for me to hold on to a grudge for any length of time. God's forgiveness was instant and so should mine be. I opened my Bible and read. It wasn't long before I was downstairs apologizing to the whole family. God has forgiven us for so much, so when we take it into perspective, how can we not forgive each other?

Are you holding anything against someone today? If so, exercise childlike faith and let it go!

NOTES

"You are not alone. I am with you always. Practice being mindful of my presence and what I say about you! My love is never shaken by trouble. You can take refuge in me and know that the sun will come out and you will laugh again. Choose to believe that I am greater and together we are more than conquerors."

Week Forty-six

Rediscover Yourself

*"So do not fear, for I am with you; do not be dismayed, for I am your God.
I will strengthen you and help you; I will uphold you with my
righteous right hand."*

—Isaiah 41:10

Depression drains you mentally, spiritually, and physically. Even energetic people who were once full of hope and drive can have trouble getting out of bed when suffering with depression. While overcoming depression isn't quick or easy, it's not impossible. These are steps you can take to rediscover yourself and start living again.

1. Say what God says about you. Find Scriptures that you can repeat throughout the day. Say them out loud. Write positive affirmations from God's Word on paper and post them throughout your home in places you will look often.

2. Set the stage. Keep background music on in your home that sets the stage for a peace-filled and positive atmosphere.

3. Get outside. Make sure you're seeing daylight for at least 30 minutes a day either through sunlight or a light made for imitating the effects of sunlight.

4. Look ahead. Let go of regret and stop looking at your past. Write down a list of dreams you have for your future.

5. Exercise. Getting in 30 minutes of cardio activity at least three times a week means those "runner's high" endorphins get released regularly and help you work through and release stress.

6. Sleep. Turn your lights down and try to go to bed at the same time every night. Remember, a tired body and a quiet mind are the requirements for quality sleep. Turn the television off and engage in calming, quiet activities like reading, taking a warm bath, etc.

7. Socialize. Spend *face* time, not Facebook time, with close friends and family. Have some fun! Keep it simple and go to dinner, a movie, a sporting event, or just grab a cup of coffee together.

Pay attention to those times when you tend to dwell on the negatives in your life—both real or imagined—and stop them. It takes work and persistence, but you can tell yourself to stop rehearsing the negatives.

 NOTES

_____

_____

GOD NOTE

"Trust requires you to let go and rest in what only I can do. It doesn't relieve you of your responsibility, but it frees you to focus only on your part in obedience to me. Let go of the rest. Prayerfully leave it at my feet because I care for you and you can know I will not leave you without comfort or provision."

WEEK FORTY-SEVEN
He's in the Details

"The Lord will perfect that which concerns me."
—PSALMS 138:8

I have quoted this scripture probably more than any other verse in my life. I have a tendency to lean to my own ability and to try to fix things. And if I can't fix them, my reaction used to be consuming myself with worry over what was wrong, or speculating about what *could* go wrong so that I could pray about every situation. The problem was, there seemed to be no end to the scenarios my mind could conjure up or of needs that would arise.

Psalm 138:8 reassured me that I could rest in the Lord because *He* would take care of all the small details, the ones that I couldn't even cover in prayer! I could trust Him with the future for my life. I learned to pray with peaceful expectation and trust that God Himself was working on my behalf, handling every detail, even the ones I hadn't thought about. What a relief it was to let go of worry and self-reliance and trust God in prayer!

What concerns you today? Learn to pray this over the situations that may be troubling you and truly trust that God is at work taking care of all the details, even the ones you are not aware of. He knows and you can trust Him.

 # NOTES

"*R*ejoice in me! Get excited about the attack knowing that I align you for victory and the press is proof that your impact is greater than you suppose. After all, it's not flesh and blood that oppose you but rather the enemy who has already suffered defeat. You will rise in this pressure! You must cling to me and take rest in my promise."

WEEK FORTY-EIGHT

Overcoming Offense

"An arrogant man stirs up strife, but he who trusts in the LORD will prosper."
—PROVERBS 28:25, NASB

I have been in many situations where proud people criticized my husband or me, our family, or our ministry. It's not easy to take criticism. If we're not careful, it can sow strife and offense in our hearts toward our offenders!

I have discovered a secret to turning down these opportunities for offense, and I want to share it with you.

Exodus 14:14 (ESV) makes a life-changing promise that will drastically change the way you respond to people who speak against you. It says, "The Lord will fight for you, and you have only to be silent." Our greatest strength isn't in our *retaliation*— it's in our silence! When we get out of the way, God is able to vindicate us. God will bless you if you will back down from reacting in the flesh or letting yourself get angry and retaliating with evil. Trust Him.

Almost every time I have faced a difficult situation with people, and handled it in a right way, I have watched God bring promotion and blessing to my family and me. Is it easy to trust God to vindicate you? No, not at first; but if you realize that by doing so you will be prospered by God, then it becomes less complicated and you can actually begin to release the criticism to God with joy! Joy is there because you know God Himself is going to prosper your humble trust in Him. The proud in heart will not go away but we can turn their attacks into blessings!

You can't stop people from being haughty or critical, but you can control how you act in the situation. Pass the test of humility and trust (even when others fail it) and you will rise above the naysayers and critical mouths of the proud-hearted. Simply smile and in your heart tell God you trust Him to prosper you in spite of their attempt to get you in strife. Be kind and turn away strife.

NOTES

_____

_____

_____

_____

_____

_____

_____

_____

"My Son didn't meet every need! There were those who walked away or refused to believe and there were those whose motives were impure. If He had limitations because of people's choices, then certainly you will. Trust me with people's lives! Trust me with your identity. You are not what you do for someone. You are mine. You are only required to live in obedience to me when others do not."

WEEK FORTY-NINE

Guilty or Good Enough

> "*There is therefore now no condemnation for those who are in Christ Jesus.*"
> —ROMANS 8:1 (ESV)

I think everyone struggles with feelings of guilt at times. It seems there are always more things to do than time or energy. Needs are all around us. You want to help people, but where do you draw the line? Your boss wants more overtime. You need to be at two ballgames for your sons at the same time. Volunteer opportunities abound everywhere you turn. You haven't prayed or read the Bible today. How do you know when to say yes or when to say, "Not this time"? Then there's the guilt we battle when we feel we did something wrong or when someone is disappointed in us or expects more than we can give.

I've always found it hard to disappoint people or not fulfill their expectations, but I discovered that taking false responsibility for someone else's responsibilities doesn't fix the issue and can even make matters worse. We learned many years ago that if the enemy could wear us out with people's problems, he would. He wanted to create despair of helping anyone else. In the earlier years pastoring a church, we would drop everything to take on anyone's problem at any time, whether it was our day off to be with family or in the middle of the night. We had to learn to prioritize, to protect and to help people mature into taking personal responsibility for their problems and decisions. Strangely enough, many of the people we helped the most wanted us to do it again and again and, in the long run, ended up blaming us when we wouldn't do more.

We are called first to take responsibility for our own family and then to listen to the Holy Spirit, following His leading as to what to do in others' situations. Sometimes we keep people from stepping up and being obedient by assuming their responsibility. We create a welfare state of mind. There is a time to be a source of encouragement, to share blessings, to be an example and to share with others how we have done something, but ultimately they must make the choice to act. We can help someone with something they cannot do for themselves if it is in our power, and help give them the tools to change. Be generous and do good, but don't try to replace God in someone's life. This is no-guilt obedience to God!

NOTES

_____

_____

_____

_____

_____

_____

"What you treasure will dictate your heart and your decisions. If you treasure my kingdom, you will never lack. Possess that which is secured eternally beyond this physical realm that is perishing. Lay hold of true riches and your joy will overflow! Let go and enjoy the temporal as simply... temporal."

WEEK FIFTY

What Do You Value?

"He who loves His life will lose it, and he who hates his life in this world, will keep it for eternal life. If anyone serves Me, let him follow me."
—JOHN 12:25-26A

What do you value?

If I value myself, my time and pursue my desires more than I value and love Him, my life will be built on selfish pursuits. Ultimately, selfishness leads to loneliness. We must let go! You and I can't build a life of satisfaction and fulfillment if we are sitting on the throne of "me." We all want joy, but joy and happiness are not the same.

You can have joy by serving someone else as you serve the Father in His household. Happiness is based on circumstances that make us feel good. It can be superficial and very temporal. Joy, on the other hand, is a fruit of God's Spirit emanating from your spirit. We can possess joy in any circumstance because it is built on trust. As I let go of my life pursuit of grasping for happiness and open my hand to Him, He takes what I was greedily squeezing in my clutched fist and in return fills my heart to overflow with joy—and then fills my hands to give to others.

We have a choice: we can hold on tight to the little we have, or we can let go of it and receive an abundance of joy back from His hand.

Years ago we moved from an old farmhouse to our new dream home God had given us. Even though many things in my heart had changed, the fear of letting go or losing something was still not quite mastered. I packed almost all of our old belongings in boxes and moved them into our new home. After living in the house for a year, I finally began to unbox my possessions. There was very little of value in these boxes, to my shock and surprise. Even though I had a beautiful new home, I still had an old mind-set when I moved. I realized that my thinking had been impoverished. I had held on to that which meant nothing; and now in light of what God had given me, these things brought me no joy, only memories of lack.

We cannot be complete unless we can receive and give love. We must receive the Father's gift of love to heal us, and give it to others to truly free us.

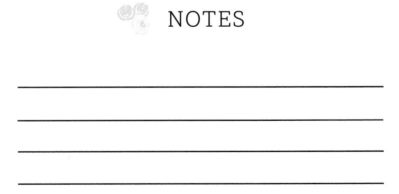 ## NOTES

_____

_____

_____

_____

GOD NOTE

"Don't idolize that which cannot save. It will destroy both you and the object of your worship. I am the God who delivers, saves and frees. Stay free from the temptation to place worship in your heart for that which taints the soul. Your heart is reserved for my love and only in our relationship can you discover true worth and value."

Celebrity Status

> "*And what do you benefit if you gain the whole world but lose your own soul?*"
> —MARK 8:36 (NLT)

We tend to confuse celebrity status in our culture with honor and forget that God is not impressed by achievements, money or accomplishments. He wants all men to come to the knowledge of salvation. What does it profit a man if he obtains the whole world but never comes to receive Jesus or God's plan for his life?

George Clooney was taping a movie while we were in Omaha, Nebraska, and we just happened to be eating in the old town section at a famous spaghetti restaurant. Our youngest daughter finished quickly and wanted to go out and watch the taping. There were huge lights and quite a production to tape the same short scene over and over.

After I finished, I went out to find Kirsten, a little concerned because so many had gathered to watch. Quite a mass of people swirled around where I was standing so that I couldn't move. The next thing I knew I was standing face to face with George Clooney. I didn't see him before or know that he was coming. I quickly said, "May I shake your hand?" (What do you say in that situation?) He said, "Why sure, darling." He shook my hand and smiled. The swirl continued to follow him as he disappeared into a building.

In that brief moment, I thought, *Wow, what was that about?* I felt the Holy Spirit say, "Pray. Pray for him right now." I didn't know what to pray, but I let God's Spirit lead me just as I had been apparently led to meet him. It made me think how we tend to idolize people whom we perceive as powerful or impressive, forgetting that they have needs too—and probably more so than many. No human being is above the need for God and His Spirit.

How many times have we neglected to pray for someone because we think they must have it all together since they have position or power? If they have been given influence with people, there is more pressure than ever. Everyone needs God.

NOTES

_____

_____

_____

_____

_____

_____

_____

_____

"I didn't send a test to you but situations will align themselves to take you off of my blessing. Don't see them as innocent but rather as defining. I am refining you to redefine you for my purpose and glory. Don't let this discourage you but rather encourage you to grow and obey when it isn't convenient. For in the faithfulness you exhibit in the small, you practice for the ability to handle the many. Get back up and keep moving forward. You are growing stronger."

WEEK FIFTY-TWO

Integrity's Voice

"*The integrity of the upright guides them, but the crookedness of the treacherous destroys them.*"
—PROVERBS 11:3 (ESV)

I was in a great hurry trying to do some last-minute shopping at one of my favorite discount stores, Home Goods. I only had a few purchases, one being a large picture. As I loaded the car, I glanced at my receipt and noticed that the clerk forgot to charge me for a flowerpot for $9.99. It seemed small, and I didn't have time to take care of it right then, so I started to drive out of the parking lot, thinking, *I will just come back later and take care of it.*

Many rationalizations began to cross my mind as I lined up behind cars waiting to leave the lot. *It was her fault for not charging me*, I thought. *It's only $9.99. I am a good customer. They've made much more than that from me.*

All of a sudden I knew what was happening. The enemy had set me up! I had been praying for God to open more doors for me in ministry and to increase His anointing on me. I turned right and circled back to the store. I ran in with the pot and my receipt and explained how the clerk had forgotten to ring it up. The clerk seemed rather surprised that I came back in. She said, "Finally, an honest person!"

As I drove away, God reminded me of Esau and how he sold his right as the firstborn son to his younger brother for a simple bowl of soup because he was hungry. I could have compromised my integrity and let go of what was most important just to avoid a temporary inconvenience, but it would have shortcut the blessing of God in my life in the long run! Don't sacrifice what is eternal for something that is temporary.

NOTES

_____

_____

_____

_____

_____

_____

_____

_____

_____

_____

ADDITIONAL NOTES